Zulus of Southern Africa

The group of people known today as the Zulus was formed about 165 years ago by the coming together of many independent clans, who had lived for centuries in the eastern coastal parts of South Africa. "Zulu" was originally the name of one small clan, which in 1816 gained a new chief, Shaka. He conquered the other clans and the nation that he thus created acquired the same name as his clan. The Zulus became feared and very powerful. The arrival of white colonizers led to conflict and eventually war: the British defeated the Zulus in 1879 and all South Africa came under white control. The native Africans had almost no political rights and were segregated from whites in a system that became known as *apartheid*. This system was opposed by the Africans, and others inside and outside the country. Today the question of full rights for everyone in South Africa is under official discussion. Throughout, the Zulus have been prominent in the struggle for equal rights.

Original Peoples

ZULUS
OF SOUTHERN AFRICA

Harriet Ngubane

Rourke Publications, Inc.
Vero Beach, FL 32964

Original Peoples

Eskimos — The Inuit of the Arctic
Aborigines of Australia
Plains Indians of North America
South Pacific Islanders
Indians of the Andes
Zulus of Southern Africa

Frontispiece *A Zulu man wearing an elaborate headdress.*

First published in the
United States in 1987 by
Rourke Publications, Inc.
Vero Beach, FL 32964

Text © 1987 Rourke Publications, Inc.

Library of Congress Cataloging-in-Publication Data

Ngubane, Harriet.
  Zulus of Southern Africa.

  (Original peoples)
  Bibliography: p.
  Includes index.
  Summary: Introduces the history, culture, and everyday life of the South
African clan, their interactions with white settlers, and opposition to the system
of racial segregation known as apartheid.
  1. Zulus — Juvenile literature.
[1. Zulus. 2. South Africa] I. Title. II. Series.
DT878.Z9N46 1987 968'.004963 87-4333
ISBN 0-086625-261-4

Photoset by Direct Image Photosetting
Printed in Italy by G. Canale & C.S.p.A., Turin

Contents

Introduction

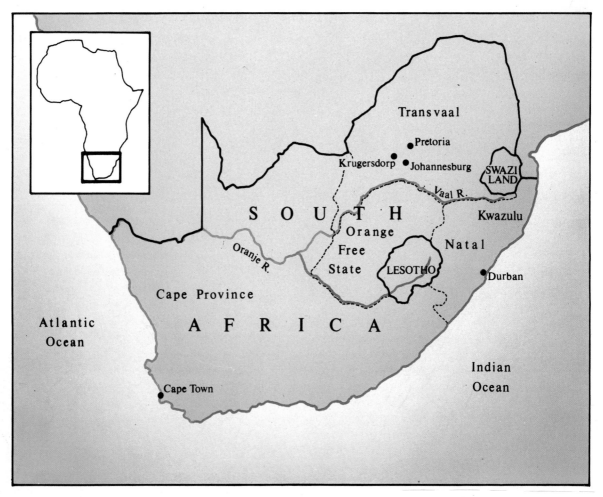

A map of South Africa today. Most Zulus live in the Zulu "homeland" of Kwazulu and in Swaziland.

The Zulus are one of the original peoples of South Africa, which occupies the southernmost portion of the African continent. The country is more than twice the size of Texas. It has a subtropical climate that favors outdoor living in all seasons.

Before the coming of white people in 1652, the western part of South Africa was mainly occupied by the Khoikhoin and San peoples. The Khoikhoin are also known by white people as Hottentots, and the San as Bushmen. The Khoikhoin lived a nomadic life. They reared cattle and sheep, but grew no crops. The San lived entirely by hunting and gathering. This meant that they had no reliable source of food, and so were much smaller and shorter than the

6

Khoikhoin, who had plenty of milk and meat to eat.

Both the Khoikhoin and the San spoke languages of a type called Khoisan, with various click sounds hardly used outside South Africa.

Along the eastern coastal and more central parts of southern Africa lived other peoples with languages of the Bantu type. These peoples resembled their northern neighbors in both culture and appearance, and like them they also grew crops as well as keeping livestocks. Thus their land could support more people than that of the Khoikhoin and San.

The Bantu-speaking peoples of the east and southeast adopted some of the Khoisan click sounds into their languages. It was the central section of these peoples, living in what is now the Province of Natal, who became known as the Zulus.

These large hats are traditionally worn only by married women.

Chapter 1 **Birth of the Zulu Nation**

The Zulu Clan

At the end of the eighteenth century, the name "Zulu" belonged to just one small clan of a few hundred people, living among numerous other clans, as they had for many centuries. Each clan was led by its own chief and occupied its own territory.

In 1816, Senzangakhona, the chief of the Zulu clan, died. One of his sons, Shaka, claimed the leadership of the clan and succeeded in establishing himself as chief.

A map of southern Africa showing the expansion of Zulu territory into the land of other clans during the Mfecane wars.

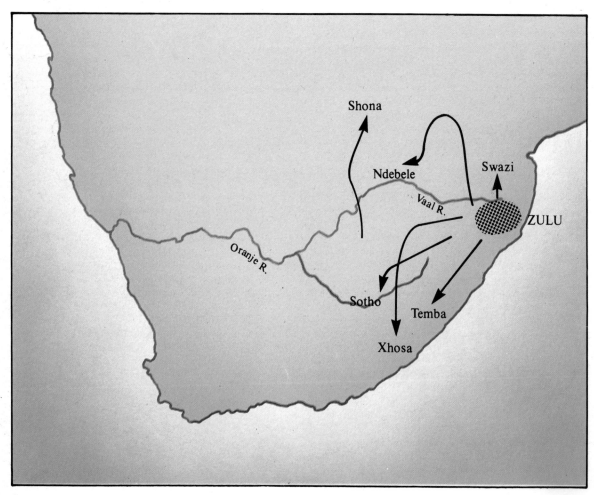

Shaka the Nation Builder

Shaka's ambition was to unite the various clans into one large nation under his leadership. To achieve this, he embarked on a program of training his warriors in new war tactics and instilling in them a sense of discipline and desire to be part of a wider nation, rather than a clan.

The new war tactics involved discarding the practice of carrying a large number of long throwing spears, which were thrown at the enemy from a safe distance. These were all replaced by a single short,

"Shaka Day" is a modern celebration to commemorate Chief Shaka.

stabbing spear called an *assegai*, which meant that warriors had to come face to face with the enemy, stabbing one after another, using the same *assegai*.

Using the new war tactics, the Zulu warriors conquered the clans around them. People who did not submit ran away in all directions to escape the Zulu conquest, and many scattered far and wide. These wars are recorded in South African history books as the *Mfecane*, or "devastating wars," which is how those who ran away remembered them.

In a period of ten years, what had been a Zulu clan, occupying a small defined territory, was transformed into a Zulu nation. It covered a large, sprawling territory that incorporated the conquered clans and the abandoned land evacuated by the fleeing clans.

Shaka was said to be ruthless in his enforcement of discipline and his desire to conquer. However, his rule was short-lived, for in 1828 he was assassinated by two of his half-brothers. As Shaka had never married and had no children, he was succeeded by Dingane, one of the assassins. Although Shaka died young, he had nevertheless managed to fulfill his great ambition of building a Zulu nation.

Left *A British officer negotiates with Shaka in 1824.*

Dingane, Shaka's successor, in dancing costume.

11

Chapter 2 **The Zulu Way of Life**

The Homestead

The Zulus did not live in villages, but in homesteads. Each homestead, or *umuzi,* was surrounded by a hedge, and consisted of several "beehive" huts built with poles and supple wood, and thatched with grass. The huts were positioned in a circle with a wide opening at one end for an entrance into the *umuzi.* In the center, a circle was fenced off with poles to form a cattle pen, where the livestock were kept at night. Each homestead had arable land around it for growing crops. Cattle were grazed on common pastures a short distance away.

An umuzi. *"Beehive" huts surround a central fenced-off area where cattle were kept.*

Herding cattle into the cattle pen.

The *umuzi* was the home of one family. A man would live with his wife—or wives, as Zulus were allowed to practice polygamy (marrying more than one wife). The man's sons and their wives and children would also be within the homestead, because a bride always joined her husband's family on marriage and remained there until the husband's father died. The son could then build his own separate homestead.

Because a bride moved to her husband's home on marriage, the husband and his relatives paid a price to her family, in the form of cattle. This practice, called *lobola,* is also common in other parts of Africa. *Lobola* is part of an elaborate wedding ceremony, and is said to indicate goodwill on the part of the bridegroom's family, and to show that they treasure the bride and will also be in a position to support her.

13

A headman was in charge of a neighborhood of several homesteads.

Administration

A homestead was the smallest unit in Zulu society. The head of a homestead was responsible for the good behavior of everybody who lived there, and was answerable to the headman for their conduct. A headman was in charge of a ward, or neighborhood, which consisted of a number of homesteads. Several wards together would make up a chiefdom, and the head of each ward reported to the chief. Similarly, all the chiefdoms together made up the Zulu kingdom, and the chiefs were answerable to the king.

The king, who represented the unity of the nation, held the land in trust for all his people and was responsible for their welfare. As this was a complex task, he delegated powers to the chiefs, who often sorted out disputes within their chiefdoms, and referred only the difficult cases to the king.

All matters concerning the national interest were dealt with in the same way. For instance, the recruitment of warriors for the army was initially the responsibility of the headman. He forwarded the new recruits from his ward to his chief who, in turn, sent them to the king.

A chief with his wives and sons.

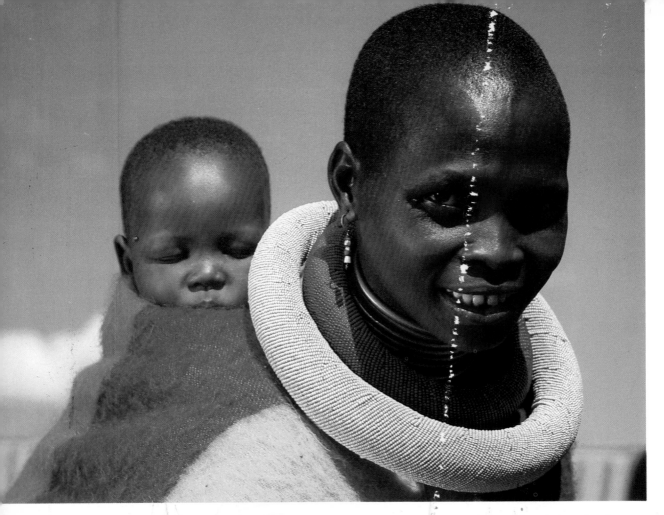

A woman and baby. Children grew up within a large family group where they had several "mothers" and "fathers."

Kinship

Kinship, or being related to someone by blood, was an important part of Zulu life. Your father's standing in society was much more important than your mother's, and it affected your social, religious and political life. You could only inherit property or rank through your father. You acquired relatives who had special obligations to you mainly through your father, too.

Such obligations were shown by using extended kinship terms. Chil-

dren used the term "father" for their own father, and also all the brothers of their father. All the wives of these "fathers" were called "mother." All the children of such "mothers" and "fathers" would then be brothers and sisters. As a result, children grew up within a large group of people who were family to them. If the real parents died, a child was never orphaned as the other "parents" took over the responsibilities.

Kinship terms also extended to people who were not blood relatives. All those who had the same surname were seen as belonging to one clan, and so could not marry, even though the direct relationship could not be traced. Anyone belonging to the mother's clan was also treated as a cousin and so was not available for marriage.

By such use of kinship terms, a wide range of people were treated as relatives. Furthermore, new relations were formed through marriage, when a clan member married someone from a distant clan. This practice of marrying outsiders, which is known as exogamy, is common in many kinship societies of Africa.

A bride, wearing a special wedding headdress, surrounded by friends and relatives at her wedding.

Religious Beliefs

The Zulus believed in an almighty and supreme being, whom they called *Umvelinqangi,* which means "the one who is always there." *Umvelinqangi* created the universe, but had little to do with day-to-day affairs. It was the spirits of dead relatives, the ancestors, who were believed to have power to bless or punish the living; so they were honored by rituals and ceremonies. The ancestors were never thought of as being in hell, but in another world, where they were believed to be happy and powerful. They were said to punish people who did bad deeds by making them suffer misfortunes.

A modern mother and children inside their hut. Taboos govern where men and women should sit inside the hut.

In daily life there were various taboos. These mainly emphasized the divisions between those who were kinsmen and those who were not. For instance, there were certain areas within the homestead where outsiders or non-kinsmen were not permitted to tread, such as where the dead were buried, or where religious rituals took place. To break these taboos was regarded as sacrilege, a grievous matter that could lead to punishment by death.

There were other taboos, which it was considered were not so serious to break. One of these related to the use of space in a hut: women always

Present-day Shembe Nazarites, a religious sect combining Christianity and the Bantu religion.

sat on the left-hand side of the doorway, while men sat on the right-hand side.

Taboos on food were connected with kinship. It was taboo to drink milk or eat any food made from it in any home other than where the family had the same surname as yours, or the same surname as your mother's family. Once again, this was another way of stressing the importance of kinship relationships.

19

An isangoma, *or witch doctor.*

Health and Healing

Illness, as the Zulus saw it, could refer not just to physical pain but also to emotional stress resulting from misfortune. So if a person died, the bereaved relatives were regarded as being ill, because of the emotional stress. To be healthy meant being in a state of physical and social well-being.

Illness could stem from natural causes such as epidemics, accidents and inherited diseases. Also there were illnesses due to breaches of proper conduct, which had annoyed ancestral spirits and caused them to withdraw their protection and blessing.

For this reason, the healers were divided into three main categories. First there was the *isangoma,* or spiritual medium (usually called a witch doctor by Europeans). The *isangoma* was often a woman. She had special contact with her ancestral

An isangoma *performs a ceremony to cure a sick child.*

spirits, which enabled her to have second sight, or clairvoyance. She underwent a long period of intensive training to gain these powers. Her main task was to diagnose the causes of diseases in order to decide on the method of cure. So if the ancestral spirits were seen to be angry, she was to indicate the reasons for their anger, in order to have them corrected.

Inyangas were herbalists who produced mixtures of herbs to cure various aches and pains. They were mainly men. They could not diagnose the cause of misfortunes, but relied on the *isangomas'* guidance.

There were also men and women who possessed one special medical skill, which was passed on within certain families. Some were bone setters; others specialized in tending wounds. There were those who had knowledge of antidotes to snake bites, and specialist midwives who helped at difficult births.

21

Land and Food

Land was regarded as a necessity of life, provided by the Creator, and so was never privately owned. However, there were rules governing its use. Rights to arable land were reserved for married people, because they alone were considered to be adults, unmarried people being regarded as minors. But if a homestead land was left unused over a long period, the chief reserved the right to reallocate it.

Land was used for growing crops and rearing livestock. Crops consisted mainly of cereals like sorghum, millet and corn, and also various kinds of beans and root crops such as cocoa-yams and sweet potatoes.

These were mainly grown and tended by women, who also collected and gathered wild vegetables and fruits.

The men mainly looked after the livestock, which consisted of cattle, goats and sheep. Apart from providing meat, cattle also gave milk. Goats were never milked. The men also hunted animals for meat.

In that warm climate, with no means of refrigeration, methods of storage were nevertheless devised. Milk was left to go sour in large gourds, then the whey (the watery part) was strained and used as a refreshing cold drink. The curdled part, called *amasi,* mixed with a cereal, formed a staple dish in every home.

When the harvest was good, surplus grain was stored in underground tanks within the cattle pen. Grain

Zulu women mixing cereals and curdled milk, which formed a nourishing meal.

Modern-day Zulu women grinding corn outside their hut.

stored in this way could last for several years and provide a reserve for periods of drought. For everyday use, grain was kept above ground in closely woven baskets.

Vegetables were preserved by blanching and drying. These, along with dried meat, were stored in large clay containers.

Zulus never developed a taste for fish, in spite of the fact that there were several well-stocked rivers and there was also the Indian Ocean. This lack of fish in their diet was probably because the land produced enough food for their needs.

23

Arts and Crafts

Both men and women made various items for the household. Women used different types of grass to weave trays, mats and baskets. They also molded large storage containers, dishes and cooking pots from clay. Men carved wood to make stools, trays, dishes, spoons and other objects. They tanned hides and skins for clothing, blankets, carrier bags, and shields to be used in battles. Only certain families, however, had the right to smelt iron ore; they made such articles as spears, knives and hoes.

Teenage girls wearing beadwork.

Intricate hairstyles were very popular. These topknots took almost an entire day to style.

Decorated articles of costume and jewelry were very popular. Colorful beads were used to make intricate patterns. This beadwork was done by women using beads obtained from the Portuguese, whose ships often put in on the eastern coast. Seashells and dried seeds dyed in various bright colors were also used for adornment. Teenage girls wore a lot of beadwork and also gave beaded items to their sweethearts. Today, the Zulus are still known for their passion for beadwork finery.

Another form of cosmetic decorative art was to make incisions on the face, forming designs, in the same way as a tattoo. Ear lobes were sometimes pierced to take a large wooden earring covered in intricate patterns. A great deal of time was spent on hairstyles. Topknots, which were popular with married women, took almost a whole day to style and knit together. Men of rank shaved their heads, leaving just a ring of hair.

Poetry was another popular artistic pursuit. Men were specialists in this, and the poems usually sang the praises of kings and national heroes. Today, we can study these poems to piece together historical information.

Growing Up

We have already seen how every child grew up in an extended family. Boys and girls were given a sense of responsibility from an early age. When infants were weaned away from their mothers, at about the age of three, they became the responsibility of their older sisters, who helped their mothers with all domestic chores. Young boys took part in herding calves, goats and sheep, while their older brothers, were responsible for the larger livestock. The herdboys also learned how to hunt and snare small game.

The older children had to protect the younger ones, and also discipline them, for they were answerable if the younger ones misbehaved.

A great deal of emphasis was placed on praising and rewarding good behavior. Children soon learned that they had to share everything. They also learned never to receive or give with the left hand, and never to look at an adult straight in the eye when speaking to him or her: eyes had to be cast down. Children were taught never to stand in the presence of their seniors, as the seniors had always to be higher in position. So when entering someone's house, a child sat

A child sweeps out a hut. Children help with chores from an early age.

down immediately as a sign of respect.

Bravery was a highly valued trait: flinching or showing pain was frowned upon. Herdboys practiced stick-fight games, which taught them how to evade blows and were also a test of how much beating they could take without flinching.

Young girls with stringed musical instruments.

In the evenings, after meals, adults and children would gather around fires to share snacks, exchange riddles, and listen to stories about the heroes of the past.

27

Chapter 3 **The Coming of the Whites**

The First Settlers

Ships passing the base at Cape Bay, under Table Mountain.

In 1488, the famous Portuguese navigator Bartolomeu Dias, sailed around the southernmost tip of the continent of Africa and discovered what later became known as the Cape of Good Hope.

From 1600, the English, the Dutch and the French set up chartered companies to trade in the East Indies. All three considered establishing a base at the Cape, but only the Dutch did

so. Jan Van Riebeeck, of the Dutch East India Company, landed at Table Bay on April 6, 1652.

The base, under Table Mountain, became important as a halfway point to provide fresh food to ships passing from Europe to the East.

Dutch and German settlers, and some French Protestant refugees, continued to arrive. From 1658, slaves were regularly imported. Society developed along very divided lines, between free whites, who had civil rights, and their black slaves, who had very few rights.

In 1795, the Cape came under British control. By then the settled white people, despite their European origin, had come to feel that they belonged first and foremost to South Africa. They called themselves Afrikaner or Boer, meaning "farmer," and they had their own language — Afrikaans — derived from seventeenth-century Dutch.

The colony's frontiers had also extended, leading to much conflict with Khoisan and Bantu peoples.

Five thousand settlers were brought out from Britain in 1820 and given farms along the eastern frontier. Most, however, became townsmen and traders. A few settled farther to the north in the land of the Zulus, at what is now Durban.

Boer men and their black slave return from a day's hunting.

Voortrekkers on the Great Trek in 1834.

Conflict with the Boers

Most Boers did not like British control and the new laws on which the British insisted. One of these concerned the emancipation of slaves.

The Boers began to move away to the north, and settled farther into the interior. This exodus of Voortrekkers, as they were known, started in 1834 and was called the Great Trek.

Most of them decided to settle in

30

part of the Zulu domain known to the whites as Natal. In 1838 the Voortrekker leader, Piet Retief, visited Dingane, the king who reigned for twelve years after Shaka, to ask for permission to reside on Zulu land.

There are different versions of what happened then, and no doubt mutual suspicion played a part. But also lack of understanding of the two ways of life existed. It seems that Retief and his party, as guests at the Royal residence, went out in the evening to enjoy the cool air, and in doing so went into places that were taboo to strangers. They were accused the next day of being sorcerers who broke taboos, and Dingane had them put to death.

The Zulus went on to attack Boer camps nearby, killing hundreds of the people in them. The survivors fought back in a series of battles, until finally reinforcements arrived from the Cape Colony and a huge battle took place on December 16, 1838, at a camp on the Ncome River. Thousands of Zulus, trapped in a ditch, were shot, their blood turning the water red.

Ever since, December 16 has been set aside as a holiday to commemorate the Boer triumph at the "Battle of Blood River." It is now called the "Day of the Covenant," from the oath sworn by the Boer army to keep holy the day God gave them victory.

The battle at Ncome River in 1834, when the Zulus were defeated by the Boers.

The Anglo-Zulu War

Although their main army had not been defeated, the Zulus realized that their weapons and tactics were no match for gunmen on horses; so they left the Boers to settle in Natal.

The British, however, annexed the new Voortrekker Republic as a Crown Colony. The Boers mostly left, joining others in the west to set up, eventually, the Orange Free State and the South African Republic known as the Transvaal.

Meanwhile, Dingane, in 1840, had been overthrown by his brother Mpande. Mpande was succeeded in 1872 by his son Cetshwayo, and the present Zulu king is his great-great-grandson.

The British wished to control the Boer republics and decided to make the Zulu nation submit to British rule. They annexed the Transvaal in 1877, and so were obliged to support Boer land claims against the Zulus.

This made Cetshwayo angry, and he began to enlarge his army. A British ultimatum arrived, demanding that the Zulu army be

The Battle of Ulundi saw the Zulus defeated by the British in 1879.

King Cetshwayo surrenders to the British.

disbanded and that a British diplomat should reside there to enforce British rule. To Cetshwayo, this meant surrendering all the power of the Zulu nation to the British and he would not meet these demands.

In January 1879 the British invaded. Despite having to use spears against guns, the Zulus put up a great fight, but in July they were defeated at Ulundi. Cetshwayo was exiled and his kingdom was divided into thirteen chiefdoms ruled by chiefs trusted by the British. They were not accepted by the Zulus however, and civil wars continued. Although Cetshwayo was restored as ruler in 1883, the unrest did not end. Nevertheless, today Zulus recognize Zwelithini Goodwill, the descendant of Mpande and Cetshwayo, as their king, even though there is no longer an independent Zulu kingdom.

A Catholic priest talks to his parishioners at the mission church in Bremersdorp.

Christian Missionaries

Although there had been some missionary activity among the Khoikhoin earlier, it was not until the end of the eighteenth century that missionaries began to arrive in South Africa in any great number. Most of them were Protestants, with headquarters in the Cape. Only gradually did their work extend into Natal and Zululand.

In 1816, Joseph Williams of the London Missionary Society (LMS) made his first Bantu converts in the Cape. Subsequently the LMS built schools, churches and hospitals for the local peoples. These churches were later absorbed into what today is known as the United Congregational Church of South Africa.

Soon after, the Glasgow Missionary Society pursued mission work that produced the Bantu Presbyterian Church.

The British settlers who arrived in the eastern Cape Colony in 1820, were accompanied by the Rev.

William Shaw, a Wesleyan minister. He founded Methodist mission stations stretching up along the eastern coast into Zululand.

Anglicans, Catholics and Lutherans also established missions. Indeed, Bishop Colenso of the Anglican Church, who was stationed in Pietermaritzburg in Natal, was a great friend of the Zulus and an adviser to King Cetshwayo right through the crisis of the Anglo-Zulu war. The first Zulu-English dictionary was produced by Father A. T. Bryant, a Catholic priest who also wrote classic books in Zulu.

Nearly all mission stations trained teachers and nurses, and other skills were also taught. Most mission schools expected those they educated to renounce traditional beliefs about ancestors, sorcery, medicines and marriage.

As successive South African governments right up until 1950 failed to provide education and health services for Zulu people, the Christian missionaries played an important role. Nearly all educated Zulu people who are now over 50 years old owe their education to the efforts of the missionaries.

A mission hospital. Missionaries continue to provide health education and medical facilities.

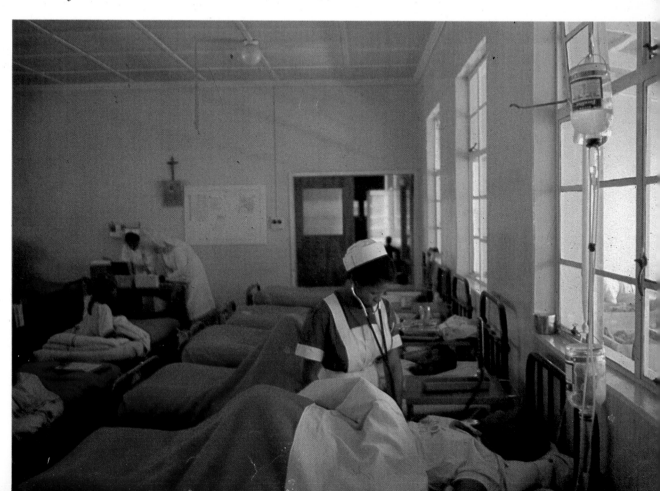

Chapter 4 **The Zulus Today**

Into the Twentieth Century

The Anglo-Boer war of 1899-1902 gave the British control over the Boer republics. After lengthy negotiations, the Union of South Africa was formed in 1910, from the four provinces of the Cape, Natal, Orange Free State and Transvaal. Although the Union was self-governing, the representatives of each province were white. Practically all the black peoples of the country were unable to vote and had no political rights.

The development of gold and diamond mining industries in the 1870s created a labor shortage. Workers were recruited from other areas, establishing a practice in South Africa of the use of migrant labor. By 1910 there were nearly 184,000 Africans employed in the gold mines.

The development of mining industries established the use of migrant black labor.

Workers' houses at Havelock mine, Piggs Peak.

The development of industries, and the participation of the Zulu people in them, placed Zulus in a new context and perspective. They found themselves part of a larger section of black peoples who were denied political rights and so needed to devise strategies to gain those rights.

It was this awareness of belonging to a wider group of deprived people that led to the formation of the African National Congress (ANC) in 1912 by Dr. P. Ka Seme, a young lawyer with an American degree. Although Dr. Seme was a Zulu with close ties to the Zulu royal family, he went beyond ethnic boundaries in founding the ANC, realizing that the political struggles of the Zulus needed to be united into a front of all the indigenous peoples of South Africa. The formation of the ANC was a political response to the 1909 Act, which created the Union but deprived the African people of any say in their future.

Apartheid

Apartheid means "separateness." It is a system based on the white domination of politics and the economy. It segregates racial groups and controls black peoples by labor regulations and by denying them political rights.

In South Africa there are four main racial groups: the whites, the coloreds (people of mixed parentage), the Asians (Indians and Chinese) and the Africans. (Since the late 1970s, Africans have been known as blacks, but are still referred to as the Bantu by some Afrikaners.)

Apartheid separates the races in all aspects of everyday life.

The struggles by blacks against apartheid have become more violent. A woman collects water in a black township after a week of rioting, looting and arson.

Many laws were passed to implement separation of these racial groups. Segregated areas were established for each race to live in. Blacks were only allowed to own land in the African Reserves (later known as homelands). Black workers had many restrictions put on them: they were only allowed to do certain jobs in certain areas, and migrant labor policies meant that many men were forced to live and work miles away from their homes and families. The races were to be educated separately.

Laws compelled every adult male black to carry a "reference book" at all times containing details about himself, which had to be produced on demand for the police.

These laws are in force today. A black may not reside anywhere outside his allocated place without permission; may not be in any white area unless he is gainfully employed (even then he is subject to a curfew at night); may not own freehold land; and may be expelled from his residence to any place if his presence is deemed undesirable.

Those who defend apartheid claim that it is the only means by which continued existence of the whites in South Africa can be safeguarded, and the only guarantee of peaceful coexistence in a multi-ethnic country. In their opinion it provides an opportunity for genuine and full development for the black peoples in their own areas.

Members of the youth wing of INkatha *march behind their banner.*

The Struggle for Rights

The response of the African people to apartheid was expressed in intensified political activities through such organizations as the African National

Congress. As a result, the ANC was banned and its leaders silenced or imprisoned. Nelson Mandela, the leader of the ANC, has been in prison since 1960. His wife, Winnie, has been campaigning on his behalf ever since. Many other leaders are also imprisoned, and some have left the country to continue their political activities from outside South Africa.

There are various other political movements that are also banned, such as the Pan African Congress (PAC) and the Black Consciousness Movement (BCM). Robert Sobukwe, the president of the PAC, died after serving a long sentence in prison. Steve Biko, president of the BCM, died under police interrogation in 1977.

The Zulu people have chosen Chief Buthelezi as their leader within the area set aside for Zulu occupation known as Kwazulu. Buthelezi organizes and consolidates the resources and political commitment of African people through a movement called the National Cultural Liberation Movement *(iNkatha yeNKubuleko ye Sizwe)*, which was set up in 1975. It has been described as the largest black political organization yet seen in South Africa, drawing its membership from the "grass roots" as well as from urban-based people living mainly in Soweto. Buthelezi has resisted government attempts to turn Kwazulu into an independent state, as has happened with some of the other black territories in South Africa. He declared: "I say that Zulus would rather die in their thousands than be forced to be foreigners in their homeland which is South Africa."

Chief Buthelezi, the Zulu leader.

41

Zulu Life Today

In spite of the widened cultural and economic horizons that education, industries, Christianity and mobility have brought, freedom of movement and of choice is tremendously curtailed by apartheid restrictions.

Nonetheless, like all black peoples of South Africa, the Zulus have made the best use of what is available to them. The Zulu university, which opened in 1960, offers degrees in Education, Law, Science and Social Sciences. A good number of graduates have sought higher education in American and British universities. Zulu life has had to change greatly to meet the demands of all these developments.

The land available cannot support the rural population. It is insufficient both in quantity and quality. Most of

A mission health clinic run by two Red Cross nurses at a chief's homestead.

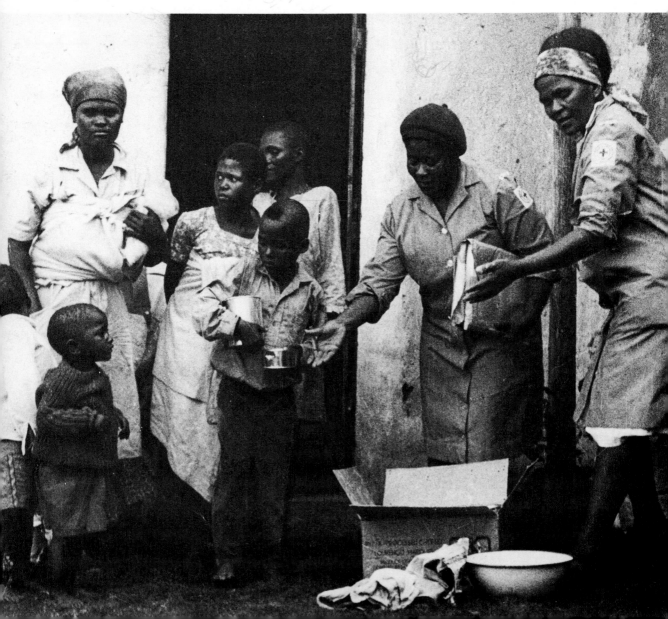

One of the many home industries that supply cheap services to local people.

A farmgirl. In Zulu society, it is the women who plant crops and do the farm work.

it is only suitable for raising livestock and not for growing crops.

Migrant labor, whereby people leave their families in the countryside to work in the cities, has become a pattern of life. Most city workers visit home once a month, but those farther away can only manage once in six months.

The kinship culture, in which relatives gave mutual support and security to one another, is now a thing of the past, due to restrictions on choice of lifestyle and the demands of a monetary economy. Mobility, owing to labor demands, encourages the dispersal of family groups. As a result, people now seek new ties to replace those of kinship. Organizations, such as church associations, give their members the support that would once have been provided by kinship.

What is the future for the Zulus? Their position in South African society results from the way that

Teacher and pupils discuss a problem during a class at a mission school.

society is organized—on the basis of conflict. Politics are dominated by racial issues, and the deprived races continually try to pressure those in power to recognize their rights.

The Zulus are prominent in this conflict because they have had a continuous confrontation with conquerors for over a century. They have never accepted a position of defeat, and have always produced able leaders. They are found in large numbers in such industrial centers as the Johannesburg area, and therefore have much influence beyond Natal.

Recently the government has at last begun to talk about moving away from apartheid and giving full rights to everyone in South Africa. Whatever happens, there is no doubt that the Zulus and their leaders will go on being at the center of events.

44

An armored personnel carrier patrols the streets of Soweto, the largest black township, after an outbreak of violence.

Glossary

Afrikaners Also known as Boers. Descended from the first white settlers, speaking Afrikaans, a language derived from seventeenth-century Dutch.

Apartheid A system of racial segregation that discriminates against black people.

Arable Land used for growing crops.

Bantu Any of the black peoples of southern, eastern or central Africa, who speak any of the Bantu languages.

Coloreds People of mixed parentage.

Exogamy The practice of marrying people from distant clans.

Homelands Areas reserved for occupation by black people.

Indigenous Originating or occurring naturally in a region or area.

Kwazulu The land set aside for Zulus in Natal.

Migrant labor The practice of recruiting labor from other areas, which means that workers have to live far away from their homes and families.

Missionary A person sent to a country to convert its inhabitants to a particular religion.

Monetary economy An economy based on currency, or money.

Pass laws Laws compelling blacks to carry a book with details of employment history, allocation of residence, evidence of tax paid, and various sorts of permits. This pass book, or reference book, must be produced on demand for the police.

Polygamy The practice of marrying more than one wife.

Taboo The forbidding of certain actions or certain social contacts.

Voortrekkers Boers who moved away from the Cape into the northern interior in the 1830s.

Glossary of Zulu Words

Amasi Thick curdled milk.

Assegai A short, stabbing spear.

Lobola The price, paid by a husband's family to the bride's family, as part of the marriage arrangement.

Mfecane The "devastating wars" fought during the reign of Shaka to expand the Zulu nation, which resulted in the scattering and dispersal of local peoples.

Isangoma A spiritual medium who is said to have second sight.

Inyanga A person who cures aches and pains with herbal mixtures.

Umuzi (plural **imizi**) A homestead made up of several houses and/or huts, housing an extended family.

Umvelinqangi The supreme being and creator of the universe, in Zulu belief.

Books to Read

Some of the books listed here may no longer be in print but should still be available in libraries.

The Zulu of South Africa by Sonia Bleeker (Morrow, 1970).

Zulu People as They Were Before the White Man Came by Alfred T. Bryant (Greenwood, 1975). Reprint of the original 1949 edition.

Shaka: King of the Zulus by Daniel Cohen (Doubleday, 1973).

Living in Johannesburg by Richard Gibbs (Wayland, 1981).

Nelson and Winnie Mandela by Dorothy and Thomas Hoobler (Watts, 1987).

We Live in South Africa by Preban Kristensen & Fiona Cameron (Watts, 1985).

South Africa: Coming of Age under Apartheid by Jason Laure & Ettagale Laure (Farrar Straus Giroux, 1980).

Zulus by John Mack (Silver, 1981).

A Zulu Family by Nancy Durrell McKenna (Lerner, 1986).

The Bantu Civilization of Southern Africa by E. Jefferson Murphy (Crowell, 1974).

Let's Visit South Africa by Bernard Newman (Burke, 1984).

Acknowledgments

The illustrations in this book were supplied by the following: Camerapix Hutchison 7, 19, 20; Camera Press 9, 17, 41, 43; J. Allan Cash 23; Bruce Coleman/ Gerald Cubitt 14, 18, 24; Leonard Lee Rue III 26; Christian Zuber *frontispiece,* 16; ET Archive 22, 29; Mary Evans Picture Library 15, 30, 31, 33; Hoa-Qui *front cover,* 13, 40; Mansell Collection 10, 11, 28, 32; Popperfoto 38, 39, 45; Royal Commonwealth Society 12, 25, 27; United Society for the Propagation of the Gospel 21, 34, 35, 37, 42, 44; Malcolm Walker 6, 8; Wayland Picture Library 36.

Index